on the radar

being a dj

Lisa Regan
and
Matt Anniss

Lerner Publications Company
Minneapolis

First American edition published in 2013
by Lerner Publishing Group, Inc.
Published by arrangement with
Wayland, a division of Hachette
Children's Books

Copyright © 2012 by Wayland

Lerner Publications Company
A division of Lerner Publishing Group, Inc.
241 First Avenue North
Minneapolis, MN U.S.A.

Website address: www.lernerbooks.com

Library of Congress
Cataloging-in-Publication Data

Regan, Lisa, 1971–
    Being a DJ / by Lisa Regan and Matt
Anniss.
    p.   cm. — (On the radar: awesome
jobs)
    Includes index.
    ISBN 978-0-7613-7775-7 (lib. bdg. : alk.
paper)
    1. Disc jockeys—Vocational guidance—
Juvenile literature. I. Anniss, Matt. II. Title.
ML3795.R416 2013
781.64023—dc23   2011051928

Manufactured in the United States of America
1 - CG - 7/15/12

Acknowledgments: Alamy: Andrew Aitchison 7,
Lebrecht Music and Arts Photo Library 26–27;
Dreamstime: Dmytro Konstantynov 1; Getty: WireImage
14; iStock: Jan Otto 23tl, 11t; Shutterstock: 28kot 31tr,
Akva 12–13, Anatema 4–5, Anky 8b, Yuri Arcurs 30l,
Ayakovlev.com 10b, Maxim Blinkov 10t, Corepics
cover, 30b, Bairachnyi Dmitry 3br, Dwphotos 2b, 28–29,
Hurricane 9, Joyfull 18, 19, Fedor Kondratenko 10c,
Kzenon 23tr, Winston Link 31b, Nikkytok 2–3, Olly 11br,
Vitechek2 20; Sara Simms 2tl, 24; Tom Thorpe 2tr, 22–23,
23tc; Wikipedia: Bigtimepeace 2c, 6, Stu Spivack 16–17,
Jay Want 17.

Main body text set in
Helvetica Neue LT Std 13/15.5.
Typeface provided by Adobe Systems.

cover stories

24

REAL-LIFE STORY
Find out how one girl's DJ dream came true.

22

FIVE-MINUTE INTERVIEW
Tom Thorpe tells On the Radar what it's like to make it as a DJ.

6

THE BACK STORY
From clubs to street corners, discover the DJ story.

28

PULL A NUMBER
Check out incredible music stats from around the world.

the**people**

the**gear**

the**talk**

HERE WE GO!

The amps are humming. The speakers are throbbing. Lights are flashing to the beat of the music. You look across the crowd and drink in the view. Thousands of people have their arms in the air and smiles on their faces. They are all there for the same reason you are—a passion for music.

The perfect track

You kneel down in the darkness and quickly flick through your record box. Being the professional that you are, you know exactly what to play next. The time is right to put on your favorite track. You carefully place your record on the turntable, drop the needle onto the grooves, and press your headphones to your ear. The smiles of the crowd turn to cheers.

Beat kicks in

Using the mixer's equalizer (EQ) controls, you turn down the bass, slide the fader across, and turn up the volume. As your favorite track kicks in, you snatch a moment to judge the crowd's reaction. Just like you, they are lost in the music. The beat kicks in, and a roar of cheers echoes around the room.

Arms in the air

You flick between tunes on two different turntables to whip the crowd into a frenzy. You feel the adrenaline pumping around your body. Your heart pounds, and you have a huge smile on your face. This is why you love your job and why the crowd loves you. They know you are going to keep them on their feet, arms raised, as you take them on a roller coaster of a dance journey. Here we go!

RISE OF THE DJ

Throughout history, people have always danced to music. The discotheques in France in the 1940s gave British dance hall owner Jimmy Savile the idea to become the world's first disc jockey (DJ). In 1947 he experimented with two turntables, and the idea quickly caught on.

Jamaican-born DJ Kool Herc is one of the pioneers of house music.

The first mixers

During the 1950s and the 1960s, people gathered at record hops to dance to the latest pop music played by a local DJ. But it was in New York City in the 1970s that the idea of a DJ as a performer took off. DJ Francis Grasso became the first person to mix records together at a nightclub. Soon dancers were flocking to clubs to hear DJs such as Larry Levan and Walter Gibbons.

Keep on moving

The first turntablists—people who use turntable tricks to make new sounds— developed in the Bronx, New York, in the 1970s. At block parties, DJs such as Kool Herc and Grandmaster Flash helped develop the style that would become known as hip-hop. They also invented scratching and beat juggling to help them stand out from rival DJs, marking the beginning of turntablism.

Making music

In 1985 in Chicago, Illinois, DJs such as Farley Jackmaster Funk, Ron Hardy, and Frankie Knuckles began to use drum machines and samplers to make their own music. Inspired by disco, they created house music—so called because it was played at a nightclub called the Warehouse. Since then, DJs have helped develop many new styles of music, from drum and bass to garage and dubstep.

Superstar DJs

DJs do not just play at clubs anymore. The Internet has allowed performances to be heard worldwide. Music festivals from Brazil to Barcelona bring clubbers together from around the world. The Winter Music Conference in Miami, Florida, and the summer months on the Mediterranean island of Ibiza, Spain, are also important dates in the diary of a DJ or clubber.

Glow sticks, bells, and whistles

The biggest change to DJing in the last 20 years has come through the development of new technology. CD turntables, DJ mixers with built-in special effects, and computer DJing software have all helped revolutionize the way people play music in nightclubs. DJs have the tools to make their sets exciting and original. The only limit is their imagination!

British superstar DJ Pete Tong has been a huge influence on DJs around the world. His radio shows are broadcast worldwide via the Internet.

7

BEAT SPEAK

Sometimes, DJs seem to have a language all of their own.

acid house
a version of Chicago house music with a repetitive and hypnotic style

battle records
tracks with good beats and samples for scratching and juggling

beat juggling
using a cross-fader to quickly flick between two copies of the same track

beat match
also called beat mix; to blend two tracks of the same speed together so that the drum rhythms are seamless and the beats match

cue up
to line up a track in the place where you want it to start playing

decks
a set of turntables

drum machine
an electronic instrument that makes the sound of drums and can be programmed to play set sequences

dub mix
a version of a track that has been stripped back to its basic parts

four-track
a piece of equipment for recording and mixing together four separate instruments

juggling
working with two samples on more than one mixer or turntable

MC
someone who jive-rhymes or raps over the top of tracks

mix
tracks that run together one after another, without a break

phasing
playing two copies of the same track together, but slightly out of time, for creative effect

promo
a promotional copy of a track sent out by a record label to advertise an artist or a song

raves
huge dance parties, often held outdoors or in disused buildings instead of in established nightclubs

residency
when a DJ is permanently based at a specific club

sampling
taking a section of a track and reusing it somewhere else

Maxi Jazz—MC for dance act Faithless— takes to the mic.

scratching
twisting a track backward and forward while altering the cross-fader

signature tune
a track that a DJ becomes famous for playing

sound system
the equipment needed to play music at a volume and quality that fills a room

set
a performance by a DJ that is made up of tracks chosen because of the way they work together

slip-cue
starting a track on its first beat by holding the record still while the turntable spins without it, achieving a near-instant start-up

white label
a promotional copy of a track given to DJs ahead of the track's official release

GLOSSARY

Scratching is most commonly tied to hip-hop music.

adrenaline
a hormone found in the human body that causes the heart to beat faster

amps
short for amplifiers; the electrical equipment that makes music loud enough to play through speakers

channels
the inputs on a mixer into which sound sources (for example, vinyl or CD turntables) are plugged

cross-fader
a control feature on a mixer used to blend the sounds coming out of two or more channels

fader
a sliding control used to alter the sound levels of a channel

house music
an electronic form of dance music developed in Chicago in the 1980s

label
a company in charge of making and releasing a record

mainstream
popular with a large percentage of the public

mixer
a piece of equipment used by DJs to mix sounds from a number of different sources

pitch-control function
a feature on vinyl and CD turntables that allows DJs to speed up or slow down music

pop music
short for popular music; widely played on radio and TV

producer
a person in charge of mixing and arranging the music to make a record

record
any form of recorded music

turntable
a device used to play vinyl records or CDs

underground
hidden or secret; not well known to many people

vinyl
a type of pressed plastic traditionally used to make records

PLAY SET

Professional DJs are techno wizards who use a range of equipment to play a set.

On the decks

Also known as turntables, decks have traditionally been used by DJs to play vinyl records. Decks designed for DJ use include a pitch-control function, which allows the DJ to speed up or slow down a record to get it in time when mixing between songs.

Mixing it up

The mixer is a DJ's most important piece of equipment. It allows him or her to move between two or more sound sources and present a seamless mix of music. Each sound source (for example, two different turntables or two CD players and a microphone) is plugged into a different channel on the mixer.

Fading across

Most mixers have a cross-fader, used by the DJ to switch between different channels. Pushing the cross-fader from one side to the other is known as mixing. The cross-fader also plays a vital role in tricks such as scratching and beat juggling.

mixer

vinyl decks

CD turntable

Technology tunes

Many DJs use computer software or digital control systems to play their sets. Software programs such as PCDJ, MixMeister, and Ableton Live let DJs mix between songs stored on a laptop computer as MP3 files. With digital control systems such as Serato Scratch Live, Torque, and Traktor Pro, DJs mix songs stored on their laptops using special control records on regular turntables. Digital control systems are very popular with turntablists.

Head start

Headphones allow a DJ to hear a record before it is played over the sound system. This lets the DJ listen to each track independently, match the beats, and cue it up. Being able to listen to a track before it is mixed in is very important to DJs, because it helps them to monitor sound levels and check whether the song is perfectly in time with what is already playing over the sound system.

IN CHARGE

Being in charge of playing music for an audience is an awesome experience. But modern DJs do even more than that. Read on to find out.

Clubbing it

Most DJs play music that people can dance to. They entertain crowds at private parties, at music festivals, and in nightclubs. DJs are passionate about music and know which songs work well as a set guaranteed to fill a dance floor. Using a range of mixing skills and some simple equipment, DJs must choose and mix the best music to keep the crowd on its feet.

Scratch that itch

Some DJs use special turntables, vinyl records, and a mixer to create routines that showcase their skills. Turntablists often battle against one another in competitions.

Turning the tables

For decades, DJs used only vinyl records. These days many DJs store their music on CDs and mix tracks together using CDJs—CD players that are designed specifically for DJs. Whatever format the music comes in and whatever equipment is used, DJing is still about playing music that an audience loves.

DJ masters

The best DJs not only play music, but they also make it. They create songs and versions of other people's records, called remixes. The world's best DJs are also music producers who find fame playing to huge audiences around the world.

DAVID GUETTA
Just genius

THE STATS
Name: David Guetta
Born: November 7, 1967
Place of birth: Paris, France
Nationality: French
Job: DJ and producer

David's fifth album featured Snoop Dogg, Lil Wayne, Usher, and Jessie J as guest artists.

Party people

Award-winning DJ David Guetta grew up in Paris, France. From an early age, he loved to listen to hip-hop on the radio and discovered house music when a Farley Jackmaster Funk track gripped his imagination. By his early teens, he was making mixtapes and organizing parties for his friends in the basement of his parents' house.

Going underground

Before he was 20, David had taken off as a DJ on the underground club scene in Paris. In the late 1980s, his love and knowledge of house music led to a slot on the French music station Radio Nova. By the mid-1990s, he was playing in the capital city's biggest clubs. In 2001 he cofounded his own record label, Gum Productions, and released his first hit single *Just a Little More Love,* featuring Chris Willis. In 2002 David followed the hit with a debut album by the same name.

Guetta blaster

Following his first album, David blasted his way into clubs around the world and into the record collections of millions of people. His next albums, *Guetta Blaster* (2004) and *Pop Life* (2007), sold more than half a million copies. His tracks often feature the biggest names in pop, from Rihanna and Kelly Rowland to Fergie and will.i.am from the Black Eyed Peas.

Career highlights

2001 "Just a Little More Love" was used on the sound track to the film *The Football Factory*

2009 released the hit "When Love Takes Over" and won two Grammy Awards

2010 won World's Best DJ at the World Music Awards show

2011 won a Grammy Award for Best Remixed Recording for "Revolver" by Madonna

2011 won three International Dance Music Awards including Best Producer

2011 released his fifth studio album, *Nothing but the Beat*

Sky's the limit

David is at the top of the list of producers that people want to work with. His remixes have been smash hits, selling millions of downloads.

David is also one of the world's best underground-to-mainstream crossover talents. As a master DJ, he appeals to a pop audience one day and plays to a club set the same night. David is one of the most popular and successful DJs of all time.

TURNING TABLES

Every year, the world's top turntablists play at the Disco Mix Club (DMC) in a competition called the DMC World DJ Championships. There are thousands of turntablists around the world, but here are some of the best:

1. Grandmaster Flash

In the 1970s in New York City, Grandmaster Flash was the first DJ to perfect the art of scratching. He was just a teenager at the time. This pioneering DJ later created beat juggling. He also built the first-ever DJ mixer with a cross-fader, which allowed him to quickly switch between records playing on two different turntables. In 1981 he released the first-ever record created using three turntables, a mixer, and a pile of records: "The Adventures of Grandmaster Flash on the Wheels of Steel."

2. DJ Rafik

German turntablist DJ Rafik grew up playing the drums before taking up DJing at the age of 13. By the age of 25, he had won a record six DMC World DJ Championship titles. He is now one of the world's most in-demand DJs and regularly experiments with new DJ techniques and equipment.

3. The Scratch Perverts

The Scratch Perverts *(right)* are the world's most famous turntablist team. They take part in competitions such as the DMC World DJ Championships, playing impressive routines using eight turntables and four mixers connected together. The Scratch Perverts are famous for scratching and beat juggling over different musical styles such as hip-hop, drum and bass, dubstep, and reggae.

4. DJ A-Trak

In 1997 DJ A-Trak shocked the turntablist community by becoming the youngest-ever winner of the DMC World DJ Championships. The Canadian was just 15 years old when he took the title, proving that if you are good enough to DJ, you are old enough!

5. DJ Cash Money

Widely regarded as the finest turntablist of all time, DJ Cash Money was the first DJ to be included in the Technics DJ Hall of Fame. After finding success in his home city of Philadelphia, Pennsylvania, in the mid-1980s, he became a worldwide star. In 1988 he won the DMC World DJ Championships.

THE CHEMICAL BROTHERS

THE STATS

Name: Tom Rowlands (left) and Ed Simons (below)

Born: January 11, 1971 (Tom); June 9, 1970 (Ed)

Place of birth: London, England

Nationality: British

Job: DJs, producers, and musicians

Student dreams

Tom Rowlands and Ed Simons first started DJing together as university students in Manchester, England, where they shared a house. First as the 237 Turbo Nutters and later as the Dust Brothers, they played a mix of hip-hop, house, and techno music in clubs around the city. In 1991 they decided to make their own music to play in their sets and in 1992 recorded "Song to the Siren." The record was then signed to the Junior Boys Own label by Andrew Weatherall, the most popular DJ-producer of the time.

Electronic masters

Their trademark sound appeals to rock fans as much as hip-hop lovers and dance music enthusiasts. To date, the band has released seven albums, has toured world-wide countless times, and has played live shows at some of the world's biggest music festivals. In 2011 Tom and Ed were invited to compose the sound track to the film *Hanna*—something that only three other DJs (Orbital, Daft Punk, and David Holmes) had ever done before.

Big beat pioneers

After leaving school in 1993, the Dust Brothers released a record called "Chemical Beats." Combining hip-hop, house, and techno, it was a huge club hit. It inspired a new wave of big beat producers such as Fatboy Slim. Following this success, Tom and Ed began to DJ around Britain. In 1995 they produced their debut album, *Exit Planet Dust*, as the Chemical Brothers. They were soon DJing worldwide. By the the end of the 1990s, the Chemical Brothers were one of the biggest electronic music acts in the world.

FEMALE DJs

Flick through *DJ* and dance music magazines and you'll find some outstanding female DJs. Yet their numbers are few in comparison to men, who dominate the industry. Until the early 1990s, few female nightclub DJs were around. Plenty of women were in bands, and big music hits often featured female singers. But somehow DJing wasn't attracting many women.

Here come the girls

All that began to change in the early 1990s. Women were finding success in various areas of dance music, and DJing

was one of them. Female DJs such as DJ Rap, Sister Bliss, and Anne Savage made names for themselves on the club scene and proved that women could perform just as well as men.

Many of the top women DJs, such as Claudia Cazacu, are trying to get other women interested in this career. "I think if there were more women active on the scene," say Cazacu, "we'd see more women at the very top." One group of female DJs set up an e-zine called *Shejay* to encourage more women to take to the decks. Cazacu is supportive of their message. "I'm not sure why fewer women choose to follow a career as a DJ because it is honestly the best job I could ever dream of."

America's Best

DJ Irene
Location: Chicago, Illinois
First DJed: 1984
Styles: Hard dance, house, trance

Baby Anne
Location: Orlando, Florida
First DJed: 1992
Styles: Breaks

DJ Heather
Location: Chicago, Illinois
First DJed: early 1990s
Styles: House

Sandra Collins
Location: Los Angeles, California
First DJed: 1989
Styles: Progressive house, trance

TOM THORPE

Club DJ Tom Thorpe has been DJing since he was 16. He regularly plays throughout Europe and Australia. He also founded the Asylum club night in Leeds, England, and is one-half of the production duo PBR Streetgang. On the Radar spoke to Tom to find out more about the world of a DJ.

What attracted you to the idea of being a DJ?

I went to my first underground club when I was 17, and it blew me away. The DJs seemed to rule the night. I was hooked there and then.

When did you first give DJing a try?

I was 16 years old when I first played on a pair of decks. I can remember it being really difficult. I really wanted to be good, so I kept on practicing.

What's your favorite music to play to a crowd?

It depends on the crowd, the party, and the size of the room. If I'm in front of a large crowd in a big room, then I play house music. For a small, intimate group, I tend to play music that is disco in sound.

What's the best way to learn DJ skills?

There is only one way to perfect your DJ skills . . . practice! The more basic the equipment you start on, the more you will understand how to play well. It's so much harder playing on poor-quality equipment (especially turntables).

What makes good DJs stand out from the rest?

Good DJs will show their passion and flair not only through their music but also with their body language when they play. If you are 100 percent into it, it shows.

What's the best way to build up your music collection?

A physical format—vinyl or CD—is best. I spend the most money on vinyl, and it is still my preferred format. I sometimes buy a track on vinyl *and* download. Then I archive the vinyl and play the download.

Who are your favorite DJs right now?

Where do I start?! I like Laurent Garnier, Maurice Fulton, Felix da Housecat, Lindstrøm, Deadmau5, Theo Parrish, Crazy P, DJ Harvey, Greg Wilson, the Unabombers, the Bays, Kenny Dope, Louie Vega, Kerri Chandeller, Daniele Baldelli— all great DJs still active on the club scene.

TURNTABLE GIRL

My story by Sara Simms (a.k.a. Ychuck)

I first fell in love with music when I was 14 years old, when my mom took me to a music store to buy my first vinyl record. By the time I was 17, I'd decided I wanted to be a DJ. I used to spend all my time on the weekends going to big parties. And when I saw great DJs playing, I couldn't wait to buy my first pair of turntables and a mixer and give it a try myself.

I found out about turntablism and the DJ battle scene from a video of an International Turntable Federation (ITF) DJ competition. This is a competition in which DJs battle for the prize of best turntablist. The video was amazing. I was completely hooked! From that day onward, I knew I wanted to be a turntablist.

My first-ever DJ gig was at a late-night party in Toronto, Canada. I performed my first turntablism set with some hip-hop records and included scratches and beat juggles. I was so nervous that I wrote down my routine on a sheet of paper so that I could look at it during my set!

Since then, I've not looked back. I'm really lucky that I am asked to play all over the world. Last week I played at a party on the beach in Cannes, France. I've also played at DJ battles in the United States, hip-hop festivals in Berlin, and lots of parties in Canada. One amazing opportunity I had was when DJ Qbert, one of the greatest living turntablists, invited me to star in a tutorial video featured on his Skratch University website.

I love being a turntablist and wouldn't do anything else. Through playing music and performing to thousands of people, I get to do what I love—for a living! It makes me so happy when I put on a great show that the crowd enjoy. It's the best feeling in the world!

♥ *Sara Simms*

FELIX DA HOUSECAT

One cool cat

Funky Felix

As a child, Felix Stallings Jr. was into funk and soul, which his father played on the saxophone. But Felix soon fine-tuned his own tastes, becoming a huge fan of Chicago house and a massive admirer of the rock idol Prince. By the age of 14, Felix was making house music at home on his four-track recording equipment.

Study leave

At the age of 15, Felix got his first break when he met a pioneer of acid house, DJ Pierre, who helped him make his first single, "Phantasy Girl." Felix's parents had other plans for their son, however. They encouraged him to enroll at Alabama State University and leave his turntables and house music behind. Their plans didn't work out.

Who's that cat?

Felix's girlfriend was into house music, and as a result, Felix began mixing and producing when he left school. DJ Pierre helped him release the record "Thee Dawn" in 1992, which gave him his big break in Europe. Felix then formed

Radikal Fear Records—one of the top house labels in the world. He released more of his own hits, as well as those by artists such as DJ Sneak and Armando. People know Felix as Felix da Housecat, but he has also recorded under many names including Aphrohead, Thee Maddkatt Courtship, and Sharkimaxx.

Alias Felix

Felix's music can be heard on the sound tracks to video games, TV shows, and movies. He has remixed tracks for P. Diddy, "Jack U"; Madonna, "American Life"; Kylie, "Where Is the Feeling?"; and Britney Spears, "Toxic." It is hard to keep up with just how many amazing tunes he is responsible for (his aliases make it tricky!), but industry insiders agree that the funky feline has created some of dance music's greatest-ever tracks.

Felix's career just keeps on going from strength to strength.

THE STATS

Name: Felix da Housecat (Felix Stallings Jr.)
Born: August 25, 1971
Place of birth: Chicago, Illinois
Nationality: American
Job: Producer and DJ

Career highlights

1995 released his first full-length album, *Alone in the Dark*

2001 won Best Album for *Kittenz and Thee Glitz* at the Muzik Awards, beating electro stalwarts Daft Punk

2003 nominated for a Grammy Award for remix of "Lost Love"

2011 released the album, *Son of Analogue*, for free on the cover of *Mixmag* magazine

HIT RECORDS

3

The age that the toddler who would become DJ Jack started playing his dad's records. At six, he played his first gig. He holds three world records for being the youngest DJ in the world.

10,000

The average number of clubbers who dance the night away at the world's biggest dance club, Privilege, in Ibiza, Spain.

4

The number of decks American house DJ Donald Glaude uses to mix his sets.

250,000

The number of revelers who flocked to Fatboy Slim's Big Beach Boutique DJ set in Brighton, England, in 2002.

1,400+

The number of DJs and artists at the world-famous Winter Music Conference in Miami, Florida, in 2011.

10

The average number of hours in DJ-producer Danny Tenaglia's sets. He regularly plays from midnight until 10 A.M. the next day!

27

The number of gigs in 25 days. That is DJ Tiësto's record. In 2010 he performed an exhausting 21 consecutive gigs in 21 days.

$470,000

The amount of money top club DJs can make in just one year.

50,000

The estimated number of records owned by club and radio DJ Gilles Peterson.

MUSICIANS OR JUKEBOXES?

Many people believe that DJing is an art form in its own right. As a result, DJs should be treated as musicians. They argue that:

1. The best DJs have a wide musical knowledge and an understanding of what makes people dance. They use these skills to take their audiences on a journey through different styles, sounds, and rhythms.
2. Like other musicians, many DJs use their creativity and skill to give their audience an enthralling live performance.
3. Turntablists have proved that two turntables, a mixer, and a pile of records can be used as an instrument. Creative turntablists are always looking for ways to create new sounds and musical effects using simple equipment.
4. DJing has changed the way people make music. DJs were the first to use loops and samples as the basis of records. Bands, singers, and producers routinely use samples in their music.

AGAINST

Other people believe that DJing is nothing more than putting tracks on a machine and that DJs should not be regarded as artists. They argue that:

1. All that is required to DJ is a basic grasp of mixing music, something that can be learned in a few days.
2. Most DJs are nothing more than glorified "jukeboxes." All DJs do is play recorded music.
3. DJs who play music made by other people are not doing anything creative. They are making money from the hard work of real musicians, singers, and songwriters.
4. The success of the music video game *DJ Hero* proves that DJing is little more than matching beats. Music made by DJs is simple, repetitive, and formulaic. It is of less musical value than songs written by musicians.

RIGHT OR WRONG?

DJing can be a great platform for musical creativity and inventiveness, offering people the opportunity to take music in new directions. However, DJs can be considered artists only if they actually create something new rather than just play other people's music. A lazy DJ is a bad DJ!

GET MORE INFO

Books

Anniss, Matt. *DJ-ing*. New York: Rosen Publishing Company, 2010. Learn about DJs and DJing.

Covington, Priest. *Go DJ!* Atlanta: DJ Priest, 2011. Written by an 11-year-old DJ, this book shows that hard work is necessary for being successful.

Websites

Disc Jockey 101
http://www.discjockey101.com/
Check out this website for tips useful for DJs just starting out.

DJMag
http://www.djmag.com/
This online magazine will keep you up-to-date on what there is to know about current DJ trends.

http://www.djpriest.net/
Visit the website of the 11-year-old DJ Priest, "the King of Clean."

DMC DJ World Championships Website
http://www.dmcdjchamps.com/
Every year, DJs come together to compete in the DMC DJ Championships. This website has information on the competitors and includes photos and videos of DJs performing.

Grandmaster Flash
http://grandmasterflash.com/
Check out the official website for Grandmaster Flash, the man who is known for first using the "scratching" technique.

Shejay
http://www.shejay.net/index.php
This website was created to promote female DJs and includes bios and news articles about them.

INDEX